~A BINGO BOOK~

# United States Geography Bingo Book

## COMPLETE BINGO GAME IN A BOOK

Written By Rebecca Stark

**Educational Books 'n' Bingo**

ISBN 978-0-87386-467-1

**Educational Books 'n' Bingo**

Printed in the U.S.A.

# UNITED STATES GEOGRAPHY BINGO
## Directions

**INCLUDED:**

List of Terms

Templates for Additional Terms and Clues

2 Clues per Term

30 Unique Bingo Cards

Markers

1. **Either cut apart the book or make copies of ALL the sheets. You might want to make an extra copy of the clue sheets to use for introduction and review. Keep the sheets in an envelope for easy reuse.**

2. Cut apart the call cards with terms and clues.

3. Pass out one bingo card per student. There are enough for a class of 30.

4. Pass out markers. You may cut apart the markers included in this book or use any other small items of your choice.

5. Decide whether or not you will require the entire card to be filled. Requiring the entire card to be filled provides a better review. However, if you have a short time to fill, you may prefer to have them do the just the border or some other format. Tell the class before you begin what is required.

6. There are 50 topics. Read the list before you begin. If there are any topics that have not been covered in class, you may want to read to the students the topic and clues before you begin.

7. There is a blank space in the middle of each card. You can instruct the students to use it as a free space or you can write in answers to cover topics not included. Of course, in this case you would create your own clues. (Templates provided.)

8. Shuffle the cards and place them in a pile. Two or three clues are provided for each topic. If you plan to play the game with the same group more than once, you might want to choose a different clue for each game. If not, you may choose to use more than one clue.

9. Be sure to keep the cards you have used for the present game in a separate pile. When a student calls, "Bingo," he or she will have to verify that the correct answers are on his or her card AND that the markers were placed in response to the proper questions. Pull out the cards that are on the student's card keeping them in the order they were used in the game. Read each clue as it was given and ask the student to identify the correct answer from his or her card.

10. If the student has the correct answers on the card AND has shown that they were marked in response to the *correct questions,* then that student is the winner and the game is over. If the student does not have the correct answers on the card OR he or she marked the answers in response to *the wrong questions,* then the game continues until there is a proper winner.

11. If you want to play again, reshuffle the cards and begin again.

### Have Fun!

# TERMS INCLUDED

**STATES**

ALABAMA

ALASKA

ARIZONA

ARKANSAS

CALIFORNIA

COLORADO

CONNECTICUT

DELAWARE

FLORIDA

GEORGIA

HAWAII

IDAHO

ILLINOIS

INDIANA

IOWA

KANSAS

KENTUCKY

LOUISIANA

MAINE

MARYLAND

MASSACHUSETTS

MICHIGAN

MINNESOTA

MISSISSIPPI

MISSOURI

MONTANA

NEBRASKA

NEVADA

NEW HAMPSHIRE

NEW JERSEY

NEW MEXICO

NEW YORK

NORTH CAROLINA

NORTH DAKOTA

OHIO

OKLAHOMA

OREGON

PENNSYLVANIA

RHODE ISLAND

SOUTH CAROLINA

SOUTH DAKOTA

TENNESSEE

TEXAS

UTAH

VERMONT

VIRGINIA

WASHINGTON

WEST VIRGINIA

WISCONSIN

WYOMING

**CAPITAL**

DISTRICT OF COLUMBIA

**OTHER TOPICS**

AMERICAN SAMOA

APPALACHIAN MOUNTAINS (APPALACHIA)

GREAT LAKES

GREAT PLAINS

GUAM

MISSISSIPPI RIVER

PUERTO RICO

ROCKY MOUNTAINS

U.S. VIRGIN ISLANDS

# Additional Terms

Choose as many additional terms as you would like and write them in the squares.
Repeat each as desired.
Cut out the squares and randomly distribute them to the class.
Instruct the students to place their square on the center space of their card.

|  |  |  |  |  |
|---|---|---|---|---|
|  |  |  |  |  |
|  |  |  |  |  |
|  |  |  |  |  |
|  |  |  |  |  |
|  |  |  |  |  |
|  |  |  |  |  |

United States Geography Bingo

# Clues for
# Additional Terms

Write three clues for each of your additional terms.

| | |
|---|---|
| _____<br><br>1.<br><br>2.<br><br>3. | _____<br><br>1.<br><br>2.<br><br>3. |
| _____<br><br>1.<br><br>2.<br><br>3. | _____<br><br>1.<br><br>2.<br><br>3. |
| _____<br><br>1.<br><br>2.<br><br>3. | _____<br><br>1.<br><br>2.<br><br>3. |

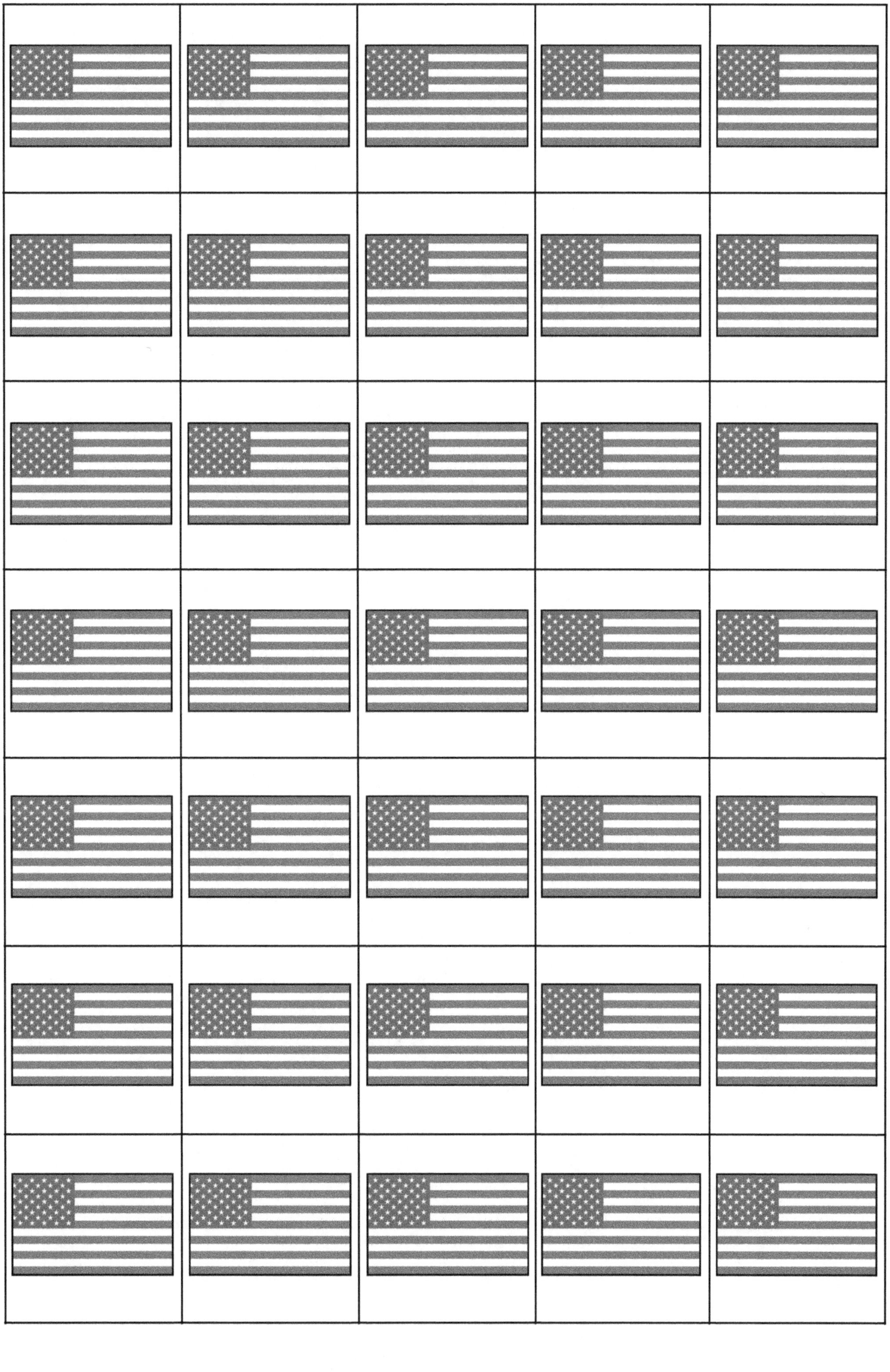

## ALABAMA

1. The capital of this state is Montgomery, but its largest city is Birmingham. Mobile, its third largest city, is located on the Gulf of Mexico.
2. Known as the "Heart of Dixie," this southern state is a large producer of cotton.
3. It is bordered by Florida, Georgia, Mississippi and Tennessee.

## ALASKA

1. The capital of this state is Juneau, but its largest city is Anchorage.
2. It is the largest state in the United States in area but only 48th in population.
3. Part of this state crosses the Arctic Circle and it is sometimes called the "Land of the Midnight Sun" because days are so long in the summer.

## ARIZONA

1. The capital and largest city of this state is Phoenix.
2. Its famous nickname is the "Grand Canyon State," but it is also called the "Copper State" because of its mineral wealth.
3. The Colorado River flows through the Grand Canyon in this state.

## ARKANSAS

1. The capital and largest city of this state is Little Rock.
2. Its official nickname is the "Natural State" because of the natural beauty of its lakes and streams and its abundant wildlife.
3. Hot Springs National Park, the oldest federal reserve in the United States, is located here.

## CALIFORNIA

1. The capital of this state is Sacramento, but its largest city is Los Angeles. This is the most populous state in the United States and the third largest in area.
2. This large state on the west coast is known for the production of grapes.
3. Its nickname is the "Golden State" and its state tree is the redwood.

## COLORADO

1. The capital and largest city of this state is Denver.
2. This state is bordered by Arizona, Kansas, Nebraska, New Mexico, Oklahoma, Utah, and Wyoming.
3. Mesa Verde in this state includes about 600 cliff dwellings.

## CONNECTICUT

1. The capital of this state is Hartford, but its largest city is Bridgeport.
2. Along with Maine, New Hampshire, Vermont, Massachusetts, and Rhode Island, this state is part of New England.
3. It is called the "Constitution State."

## DELAWARE

1. The capital of this state is Dover, but its largest city is Wilmington.
2. The state's nickname is the "First State" because it was the first of the 13 original states to ratify the United States Constitution.
3. This is the second-smallest state in the United States.

## FLORIDA

1. The capital of this state is Tallahassee, but its largest city is Jacksonville.
2. The Everglades, the largest subtropical wilderness in the United States, is located in this state.
3. This state's official nickname is the "Sunshine State." It is known for its production of oranges.

United States Geography Bingo

## GEORGIA

1. The capital and largest city of this state is Atlanta.
2. This Southern state's official nickname is the "Peach State."
3. The 3 largest cities after Atlanta are Augusta, Columbus and Savannah.

| | |
|---|---|
| **HAWAII**<br>1. The capital and largest city of this state is Honolulu.<br>2. Known as the "Aloha State," it became the 50th state in the Union on August 21, 1959.<br>3. This state is located on an archipelago in the central Pacific Ocean. | **IDAHO**<br>1. The capital and largest city of this state is Boise.<br>2. Best known for its potatoes, this state's other important agricultural products include cattle, dairy products, wheat, sugar beets, and barley.<br>3. The Snake River flows from Wyoming into this state. |
| **ILLINOIS**<br>1. The capital of this state is Springfield, but its largest city is Chicago.<br>2. It is the most populous state in the Midwest. Its nickname is the "Prairie State." It is also known as the "Land of Lincoln."<br>3. It borders Indiana, Iowa, Michigan, Kentucky, Missouri, Wisconsin and Lake Michigan. | **INDIANA**<br>1. The capital and largest city of this state is Indianapolis.<br>2. It is known as the "Hoosier State."<br>3. The Wabash River cuts the state in half from northeast to southwest before flowing south, mostly along the border with Illinois. |
| **IOWA**<br>1. Its capital and largest city is Des Moines.<br>2. Known officially as the "Hawkeye State," this state is bordered on the West by the Missouri River and on the east by the Mississippi River.<br>3. This state ranks number one in corn production and is also known for its production of soybeans. | **KANSAS**<br>1. The capital of this state is Topeka, but its largest city is Wichita.<br>2. This state is called the "Sunflower State." Sunflower and wheat are its most important crops.<br>3. This state is bordered by Nebraska, Missouri, Oklahoma and Colorado. |
| **KENTUCKY**<br>1. The capital of this state is Frankfort, but its largest city is Lexington-Fayette.<br>2. It is known as the "Bluegrass State" because in the spring the grass produces bluish-purple buds.<br>3. The annual horse race known in its shortened form as the "Derby" has been held in this state since 1875. | **LOUISIANA**<br>1. The capital of this state is Baton Rouge, but its largest city is New Orleans.<br>2. Its nickname is the "Pelican State" and the official state bird is the brown pelican.<br>3. Its largest city, New Orleans, is known for jazz. |
| **MAINE**<br>1. The capital of this state is Augusta, but its largest city is Portland.<br>2. Known as the "Pine Tree State," this state has more than 17 million acres of forests.<br>3. It is the northernmost state in New England and the easternmost state in the contiguous United States. | **MARYLAND**<br>1. The capital of this state is Annapolis, but its largest city is Baltimore.<br>2. Chesapeake Bay in this state is the largest freshwater estuary in the world. It almost divides the state in half.<br>3. The land occupied by Washington, DC, was originally part of this state. |

| | |
|---|---|
| **MASSACHUSETTS**<br>1. The capital and largest city of this state is Boston.<br>2. It has two nicknames: "Bay State" because of its proximity to several large bays and the "Old Colony State" in honor of Plymouth colony.<br>3. The Charles River, although relatively short, is the most populous river basin in New | **MICHIGAN**<br>1. The capital of this state is Lansing, but its largest city is Detroit.<br>2. This state has 2 nicknames: the "Wolverine State" and the "Great Lake State." Its shores touch four of the five Great Lakes, and it has more than 11,000 inland lakes.<br>3. This state is known for the production of motor vehicles and their parts. |
| **MINNESOTA**<br>1. The capital of this state is St. Paul, but its largest city is Minneapolis. The metropolitan area of these cities is known as the "Twin Cities."<br>2. It is called the "North Star State" and the "Land of 10,000 Lakes," although it really has 12,000.<br>3. This Midwestern state is the second | **MISSISSIPPI**<br>1. The capital and largest city of this state is Jackson.<br>2. It is nicknamed the "Magnolia State."<br>3. Located in the Deep South, the name of this state comes from the great river that flows along its western boundary. That river is the second longest in the country. |
| **MISSOURI**<br>1. The capital of this state is Jefferson City, but its largest city is Kansas City. The 4 largest metropolitan areas are St. Louis, Kansas City, Springfield, and Columbia.<br>2. Its nickname is the "Show Me State."<br>3. The Gateway Arch in St. Louis is not only the tallest monument in this state but also in the U.S. | **MONTANA**<br>1. The capital of this state is Helena, but its largest city is Billings.<br>2. Its nickname is the "Treasure State"because of the importance of mining in this state. Other nicknames include "Land of Shining Mountains" and "Big Sky Country.<br>3. Glacier National Park is located here. |
| **NEBRASKA**<br>1. The capital of this state is Lincoln, but its largest city is Omaha.<br>2. Its official nickname is the "Cornhusker State."<br>3. The Platte River drains a large portion of the central Great Plains in this Midwestern state as well as the eastern Rocky Mountains in Colorado and Wyoming. | **NEVADA**<br>1. The capital of this state is Carson City, but its largest city is Las Vegas.<br>2. It is called the "Silver State" because of its large silver-mine industries. Other nicknames include the "Sage State" and the "Sagebrush State."<br>3. Much of the northern part of this Western state is within the Great Basin, and the south- |
| **NEW HAMPSHIRE**<br>1. The capital of this state is Concord, but its largest city is Manchester.<br>2. Its nickname is the "Granite State" because it once had a large industry surrounding the quarrying of granite. Its state motto is "Live Free or Die."<br>3. This New England state is known for having the first primary in the presidential-election<br>United States Geography Bingo | **NEW JERSEY**<br>1. The capital of this state is Trenton, but its largest city is Newark.<br>2. This Mid-Atlantic state is known as the "Garden State."<br>3. This Mid-Atlantic state has 127 miles of white sand beaches. The most famous beach resort in this state is Atlantic City.<br><br>© **Barbara M. Peller** |

| NEW MEXICO | NEW YORK |
|---|---|
| 1. The capital of this state is Santa Fe, but its largest city is Albuquerque.<br>2. Taos Pueblo, a multi-storied residential complex of reddish-brown adobe is in ___. It was designated a World Heritage Site in 1992.<br>3. This Southwestern state's automobile license plates have the words "Land of Enchantment" on them. | 1. The capital of this state is Albany, but it is not the largest city. Its largest city is also the largest city in the country.<br>2. This state's nickname is the "Empire State."<br>3. Tourists visiting the largest city in this state often go to the Statue of Liberty, Ellis Island and the Empire State Building. |
| **NORTH CAROLINA** | **NORTH DAKOTA** |
| 1. The capital of this state is Raleigh, but its largest city is Charlotte.<br>2. The nickname of this southeastern state is the "Tar Heel State."<br>3. Pamlico Sound in ___ is the largest lagoon along the eastern coast; it is separated from the Atlantic Ocean by the Outer Banks, a row of sandy barrier islands, including Cape Hatteras. | 1. The capital of this state is Bismarck, but its largest city is Fargo.<br>2. Its official nickname is the "Peace Garden State." It is also called "Flickertail State."<br>3. Lake Sakakawea is a reservoir in the Missouri River basin in the central part of ___. It is the 3rd largest man-made lake in the U.S, after Lake Mead and Lake Powell. |
| **OHIO** | **OKLAHOMA** |
| 1. The capital and largest city of this state is Columbus.<br>2. Its nickname is the "Buckeye State."<br>3. This Midwestern state borders Pennsylvania; Michigan; Ontario, Canada; Indiana; Kentucky; and West Virginia. It has the highest population density of any state *not* on the eastern seaboard. | 1. Its capital and largest city is Oklahoma City.<br>2. This state in the South Central region of the United States is called the "Sooner State" after the people who lined up early when the Indian Territory was opened to settlers in 1889.<br>3. Tulsa, the second-largest city in this state, held the nickname "Oil Capital of the World" for much of the 20th century. |
| **OREGON** | **PENNSYLVANIA** |
| 1. The capital of this state is Salem, but its largest city is Portland.<br>2. The nickname of this state in the Pacific Northwest is the "Beaver State."<br>3. The Columbia River forms much of the border between this state and the state of Washington. | 1. The capital of this state is Harrisburg, but its largest city is Philadelphia.<br>2. The nickname of this Mid-Atlantic state is the "Keystone State."<br>3. Its 10 most populated cities are Philadelphia, Pittsburgh, Allentown, Erie, Reading, Scranton, Bethlehem, Lancaster, Altoona, and Harrisburg. |
| **RHODE ISLAND** | **SOUTH CAROLINA** |
| 1. Providence is the capital and largest city of __.<br>2. The nickname of this state is the "Ocean State." Another nickname,"Plantation State," is derived from the state's official full name. (Although it is the smallest state, it has the longest official name.)<br>3. Narragansett Bay in this state forms New England's largest estuary. | 1. The capital and largest city of this state is Columbia.<br>2. The nickname of this Southern state, the "Palmetto State," refers to its official state tree.<br>3. The Savannah River forms most of the border between this state and Georgia. |

United States Geography Bingo

| | |
|---|---|
| **SOUTH DAKOTA**<br>1. The capital of this state is Pierre, but its largest city is Sioux Falls.<br>2. It is called "Mount Rushmore State" because of the granite monument sculpted by Gutzon Borglum in the Black Hills region of the state.<br>3. The borders of this Midwestern state include North Dakota, Nebraska, Iowa, Minnesota, Wyoming and Montana. | **TENNESSEE**<br>1. The capital of this state is Nashville, but its largest city is Memphis.<br>2. This Southern state is often called the "Volunteer State."<br>3. It ties Missouri in the number of states it borders. It borders Kentucky, Virginia, North Carolina, Georgia, Alabama, Mississippi, Arkansas, and Missouri. |
| **TEXAS**<br>1. The capital of this state is Austin, but its largest city is Houston.<br>2. Known as the "Lone Star State," this is the second largest state in the United States. The first cowboys, called *vaqueros,* were from here.<br>3. It is located at the southernmost part of the Great Plains. The Rio Grande, Red River and Sabine River are natural state borders. | **UTAH**<br>1. The capital and largest city of this state is Salt Lake City.<br>2. The beehive is the official state emblem of this western state. One of its natural wonders is the Delicate Arch, which is made of sandstone.<br>3. It is one of the Four Corners states; the others are Colorado, New Mexico, and Arizona. |
| **VERMONT**<br>1. The capital of this state is Montpelier, but its largest city is Burlington.<br>2. Its nickname is the "Green Mountain State." It is the only New England state without a coastline along the Atlantic Ocean.<br>3. This New England state is known for its production of maple syrup. | **VIRGINIA**<br>1. The capital of this state is Richmond, but its largest city is Virginia Beach.<br>2. Its nickname is "Old Dominion State."<br>3. Popular historical tourist attractions in this Southern state include Jamestown, Yorktown and Colonial Williamsburg. |
| **WASHINGTON (STATE)**<br>1. The capital of this state is Olympia, but its largest city is Seattle.<br>2. The nickname of this state in the Pacific Northwest is the "Evergreen State" because of its abundant evergreen forests.<br>3. Mount Rainier is located in this state. | **WEST VIRGINIA**<br>1. Its capital and largest city is Charleston.<br>2. It is called the "Mountain State." It is the only state in which all regions are mountainous.<br>3. It became a state during the Civil War when it separated from a state that had seceded. |
| **WISCONSIN**<br>1. The capital of this state is Madison, but its largest city is Milwaukee.<br>2. This state is called the "Badger State."<br>3. This Midwestern state is known for its production of cheese and other dairy products. | **WYOMING**<br>1. The capital and largest city of this state is Cheyenne.<br>2. It is known as the "Equality State" because women in this state were the first in the United States to gain the right to vote, to serve on juries and to hold public office.<br>3. Although this Western state is the tenth largest by size, it is the least populous state. |

United States Geography Bingo

| DISTRICT OF COLUMBIA | AMERICAN SAMOA |
|---|---|
| 1. Also called Washington, this is the capital of the United States of America.<br>2. The centers of all 3 branches of the Federal government of the U.S. are in the ___.<br>3. Located on the banks of the Potomac River, it is bordered by Virginia to the southwest and Maryland to the northwest, northeast, & southeast. | 1. This unincorporated territory of the United States is located in the South Pacific Ocean.<br>2. Pago Pago Town, in the island of Tutuila, is a tourist destination in this territory.<br>3. This group of six Polynesian islands in the South Pacific is the southernmost territory of the United States. |
| **APPALACHIAN MOUNTAINS (APPALACHIA)** | **GREAT LAKES** |
| 1. This vast system of mountains is located in eastern North America.<br>2. The Allegheny Mountains are part of this vast mountain range.<br>3. Although coal mining is the industry often associated with this region, coal is mined only in some portions of the area. | 1. They form the largest group of freshwater lakes on Earth.<br>2. In order of size they are Lake Superior, Lake Huron, Lake Michigan, Lake Erie, and Lake Ontario.<br>3. Lake Superior, the largest of them, has the largest surface area of any freshwater lake in the world. |
| **GREAT PLAINS** | **GUAM** |
| 1. __ is the name given to the broad expanse of prairie and steppe east of the Rocky Mountains.<br>2. This area covers parts of Colorado, Kansas, Montana, Nebraska, New Mexico, North Dakota, Oklahoma, South Dakota, Texas and Wyoming.<br>3. The American bison is the most famous animal of this region. | 1. This island in the North Pacific Ocean is a U.S. territory. It is the largest and southernmost island in the Mariana Islands archipelago.<br>2. The military installation here is a strategically important U.S. base in the Pacific.<br>3. It was ceded to the U.S. by Spain in 1898. In 1941 it was captured by the Japanese, but it was retaken 3 years later. |
| **MISSISSIPPI RIVER** | **PUERTO RICO** |
| 1. It is the second longest river in the United States. Only the Missouri River, a tributary of this river, is longer.<br>2. Its source is in Lake Itasca in Minnesota and its mouth is in the Gulf of Mexico.<br>3. A few of the many great cities along this river include New Orleans, LA; Baton Rouge, LA; Natchez, MS; St. Paul, MN; and St. Louis, MO. | 1. This semi-autonomous territory of the United States is located in the northeastern Caribbean Sea.<br>2. Its capital is San Juan.<br>3. El Yunque National Forest, a tropical rain forest, is located in the northeastern part of the island. |
| **ROCKY MOUNTAINS** | **U.S. VIRGIN ISLANDS** |
| 1. This broad mountain range in Western North America is 3,000 miles long.<br>2. The highest peak in this mountain range is Mount Elbert in Colorado; it is 14,440 feet above sea level.<br>3. The Continental Divide, which designates the line at which waters flow either to the Atlantic Ocean or to the Pacific Ocean, is in this range. | 1. This United States territory comprises Saint Croix, Saint John, Saint Thomas, and Water Island, along with smaller, surrounding islands.<br>2. Charlotte Amalie, on the Island of St. Thomas, is the capital.<br>3. They are located in the Caribbean Sea and the Atlantic Ocean, about 90 miles east of Puerto Rico. |

United States Geography Bingo

# United States Geography Bingo

| Kentucky | Alabama | Colorado | Mississippi | New Hampshire |
|---|---|---|---|---|
| Connecticut | Alaska | Virginia | Great Lakes | Mississippi River |
| Arizona | Wyoming | | District of Columbia | Georgia |
| Texas | Kansas | Wisconsin | Montana | U.S. Virgin Islands |
| Oklahoma | Maryland | Puerto Rico | Washington (State) | Vermont |

© Barbara M. Peller

# United States Geography Bingo

| Texas | Mississippi River | American Samoa | Utah | Minnesota |
|---|---|---|---|---|
| District of Columbia | Illinois | Arkansas | Delaware | Nebraska |
| Great Lakes | Maryland | | Louisiana | Wisconsin |
| Pennsylvania | U.S. Virgin Islands | Wyoming | Rhode Island | Vermont |
| West Virginia | Virginia | South Carolina | Puerto Rico | Washington (State) |

　　　　　　© Barbara M. Peller

# United States Geography Bingo

| | | | | |
|---|---|---|---|---|
| Texas | Wisconsin | Illinois | Montana | Arizona |
| New Mexico | Alaska | Hawaii | Alabama | Delaware |
| Mississippi River | Virginia | | District of Columbia | California |
| Wyoming | Idaho | Oklahoma | Pennsylvania | New Jersey |
| Washington (State) | Connecticut | South Carolina | Rhode Island | Minnesota |

© Barbara M. Peller

# United States Geography Bingo

| Wyoming | Nebraska | Colorado | Delaware | Puerto Rico |
|---|---|---|---|---|
| District of Columbia | Florida | Alabama | American Samoa | Arizona |
| North Dakota | Pennsylvania | | New Hampshire | Mississippi |
| Wisconsin | Indiana | Virginia | South Carolina | Great Lakes |
| Delaware | West Virginia | Ohio | Washington (State) | Georgia |

# United States Geography Bingo

| | | | | |
|---|---|---|---|---|
| West Virginia | Puerto Rico | Kansas | U.S. Virgin Islands | Connecticut |
| Nevada | Wisconsin | Hawaii | District of Columbia | Alaska |
| Colorado | Georgia | | New Mexico | Massachusetts |
| Vermont | Minnesota | Kentucky | American Samoa | Iowa |
| Guam | South Carolina | Arizona | Wyoming | North Dakota |

# United States Geography Bingo

| California | Nebraska | New Jersey | Minnesota | Georgia |
|---|---|---|---|---|
| Great Lakes | Kansas | Iowa | Alabama | Arizona |
| Utah | Delaware |  | Florida | Louisiana |
| South Carolina | Oklahoma | Rhode Island | Ohio | Colorado |
| North Carolina | Arkansas | Kentucky | New Hampshire | Indiana |

© Barbara M. Peller

# United States Geography Bingo

| | | | | |
|---|---|---|---|---|
| Puerto Rico | Nebraska | Massachusetts | New Mexico | Illinois |
| North Carolina | Minnesota | Maryland | American Samoa | Nevada |
| New Jersey | Mississippi | | Maine | Mississippi River |
| U.S. Virgin Islands | Guam | Hawaii | Texas | Idaho |
| South Carolina | Connecticut | Rhode Island | Ohio | California |

# United States Geography Bingo

| North Dakota | Nebraska | Louisiana | Montana | Florida |
|---|---|---|---|---|
| Nevada | Colorado | Utah | Georgia | Arkansas |
| Indiana | U.S. Virgin Islands | | Minnesota | New Hampshire |
| American Samoa | Wyoming | Texas | Delaware | Pennsylvania |
| District of Columbia | South Carolina | Ohio | Kansas | North Carolina |

United States
Geography
Bingo

| | | | | |
|---|---|---|---|---|
| Florida | Montana | Louisiana | Nebraska | West Virginia |
| Arkansas | Georgia | Utah | Colorado | |
| New Hampshire | Minnesota | | U.S. Territories | Indiana |
| | | | | |
| North Carolina | Kansas | Ohio | South Carolina | District of Columbia |

# United States Geography Bingo

| Louisiana | Illinois | Maryland | Indiana | Great Lakes |
|-----------|----------|----------|---------|-------------|
| Delaware | Minnesota | North Dakota | Kansas | Puerto Rico |
| Missouri | Guam | | Puerto Rico | Maine |
| Iowa | Vermont | Oklahoma | New Mexico | Massachusetts |
| Pennsylvania | Rhode Island | Hawaii | Texas | New Hampshire |

# United States Geography Bingo

| Texas | Montana | Great Lakes | Utah | Indiana |
|-------|---------|-------------|------|---------|
| Georgia | Arkansas | Alabama | Alaska | Minnesota |
| Oregon | Nebraska | | Mississippi | Idaho |
| Oklahoma | Great Lakes | Iowa | Rhode Island | Missouri |
| Hawaii | North Carolina | New Jersey | West Virginia | North Dakota |

# United States Geography Bingo

| | | | | |
|---|---|---|---|---|
| District of Columbia | Nebraska | Kansas | Iowa | North Carolina |
| Louisiana | Missouri | New Mexico | Maine | American Samoa |
| Nevada | Minnesota | | New Jersey | Maryland |
| Hawaii | District of Columbia | Rhode Island | Connecticut | Texas |
| Delaware | South Carolina | Kentucky | Ohio | Illinois |

# United States Geography Bingo

| Illinois | New Hampshire | Missouri | Montana | Louisiana |
|---|---|---|---|---|
| Maryland | North Carolina | Appalachian Mountains (Appalachia) | Ohio | Alaska |
| Kentucky | Massachusetts |  | Georgia | Utah |
| South Carolina | Pennsylvania | Minnesota | Texas | Nevada |
| Nebraska | Maine | Oregon | Delaware | Arkansas |

United States Geography Bingo: Card No. 12

© Barbara M. Peller

# United States Geography Bingo

| Iowa | New Hampshire | California | Missouri | Georgia |
|------|------|------|------|------|
| Colorado | Louisiana | Appalachian Mountains (Appalachia) | Maine | Idaho |
| Montana | Illinois | | Maryland | Massachusetts |
| North Dakota | Rhode Island | Florida | Oregon | Texas |
| South Carolina | Vermont | Ohio | Kentucky | New Mexico |

# United States Geography Bingo

| | | | | |
|---|---|---|---|---|
| Connecticut | Minnesota | Kansas | Maine | Guam |
| Arkansas | Kentucky | Missouri | Alaska | Nebraska |
| Iowa | Appalachian Mountains (Appalachia) | | Rocky Mountains | Hawaii |
| Vermont | Rhode Island | Oregon | Florida | California |
| South Carolina | Utah | Idaho | North Carolina | North Dakota |

# United States Geography Bingo

| | | | | |
|---|---|---|---|---|
| New Mexico | Maine | Kansas | Illinois | Montana |
| California | New Jersey | Alabama | Colorado | Delaware |
| Great Lakes | Kentucky | | Arizona | Nebraska |
| South Carolina | Missouri | Louisiana | Rhode Island | Iowa |
| North Carolina | Pennsylvania | Ohio | Appalachian Mountains (Appalachia) | Maryland |

# United States Geography Bingo

| | | | | |
|---|---|---|---|---|
| Florida | Missouri | Louisiana | Indiana | Delaware |
| Utah | Idaho | Massachusetts | Nevada | Mississippi |
| Iowa | New Hampshire | | Georgia | Maryland |
| Appalachian Mountains (Appalachia) | Arkansas | South Carolina | New York | Guam |
| Tennessee | South Dakota | Ohio | Pennsylvania | Nebraska |

# United States Geography Bingo

| Hawaii | New York | Mississippi River | Missouri | Connecticut |
|---|---|---|---|---|
| New Mexico | Delaware | Rhode Island | Mississippi | Massachusetts |
| Great Plains | North Dakota | | Rocky Mountains | Maine |
| Vermont | North Carolina | Texas | Kansas | Idaho |
| Oklahoma | Iowa | Illinois | Montana | New Hampshire |

# United States Geography Bingo

| | | | | |
|---|---|---|---|---|
| Indiana | Oregon | Arkansas | Iowa | Utah |
| Nebraska | Hawaii | Oklahoma | Georgia | Delaware |
| Maine | Idaho | | Michigan | Colorado |
| Vermont | Alabama | Rhode Island | Texas | New Jersey |
| South Dakota | Missouri | Kansas | California | New York |

United States
Geography
Bingo

| Utah | Iowa | Arkansas | Oregon | Indiana |
|---|---|---|---|---|
| Delaware | Georgia | Oklahoma | | Nebraska |
| Colorado | Michigan | | Idaho | Maine |
| | | FREE | | |
| New York | California | Kansas | | South Dakota |

# United States Geography Bingo

| Georgia | California | Great Plains | Louisiana | New York |
|---------|-----------|--------------|-----------|----------|
| New Mexico | Montana | Nebraska | Illinois | Mississippi |
| Great Lakes | Connecticut |  | Alaska | Arizona |
| New Jersey | South Dakota | District of Columbia | Puerto Rico | Michigan |
| Colorado | Tennessee | North Carolina | North Dakota | Ohio |

# United States Geography Bingo

| Oregon | New York | Montana | Missouri | Ohio |
|---|---|---|---|---|
| Arkansas | Maryland | Nevada | Oklahoma | Utah |
| Great Plains | Massachusetts |  | Wyoming | Alabama |
| West Virginia | Virginia | Washington (State) | Pennsylvania | South Dakota |
| Wisconsin | North Dakota | Tennessee | Texas | Michigan |

# United States Geography Bingo

| New Mexico | California | Nevada | Missouri | West Virginia |
|---|---|---|---|---|
| New Hampshire | Michigan | Florida | Maine | Kentucky |
| Idaho | North Carolina | | New York | Kansas |
| Oklahoma | Illinois | South Dakota | Vermont | North Dakota |
| Wyoming | Tennessee | Ohio | Hawaii | Pennsylvania |

# United States Geography Bingo

| Indiana | New Jersey | Michigan | Colorado | District of Columbia |
|---|---|---|---|---|
| Utah | Montana | Arizona | Louisiana | Alaska |
| Arkansas | Mississippi |  | Kentucky | Massachusetts |
| South Dakota | Vermont | Pennsylvania | Alabama | Connecticut |
| Tennessee | Hawaii | New York | Idaho | Nevada |

# United States Geography Bingo

| Florida | New York | Illinois | Colorado | Ohio |
|---------|----------|----------|----------|------|
| California | Oregon | North Carolina | New Mexico | Alabama |
| New Jersey | Iowa | | Washington (State) | Kentucky |
| Idaho | Tennessee | South Dakota | Great Plains | Pennsylvania |
| West Virginia | Virginia | Rocky Mountains | Oklahoma | Michigan |

# United States Geography Bingo

| | | | | |
|---|---|---|---|---|
| Florida | Oregon | Connecticut | New York | Louisiana |
| Michigan | Great Plains | Nevada | Utah | Kentucky |
| Massachusetts | Indiana | | Iowa | Idaho |
| West Virginia | Washington (State) | South Dakota | Hawaii | New Hampshire |
| Wisconsin | Wyoming | Tennessee | Montana | Virginia |

# United States Geography Bingo

| | | | | |
|---|---|---|---|---|
| Wyoming | Nevada | New York | Kansas | Michigan |
| Alabama | Vermont | New Mexico | Florida | Alaska |
| New Hampshire | Maine | | Washington (State) | South Dakota |
| Arizona | Rocky Mountains | Virginia | Tennessee | Mississippi |
| Ohio | Connecticut | Arkansas | Delaware | Wisconsin |

# United States Geography Bingo

| | | | | |
|---|---|---|---|---|
| Michigan | New York | New Jersey | Utah | Indiana |
| Oklahoma | Montana | Louisiana | Oregon | Florida |
| Vermont | Washington (State) | | Mississippi | Wyoming |
| Hawaii | Colorado | West Virginia | Tennessee | South Dakota |
| Massachusetts | Delaware | Kansas | Virginia | Great Plains |

# United States Geography Bingo

| | | | | |
|---|---|---|---|---|
| Indiana | Utah | New Jersey | New York | Michigan |
| Florida | Oregon | Louisiana | Montana | Oklahoma |
| Wyoming | Mississippi | | Washington (State) | Missouri |
| | | | | |
| South Dakota | Virginia | Kansas | Delaware | Massachusetts |

# United States Geography Bingo

| | | | | |
|---|---|---|---|---|
| New Jersey | Arkansas | New York | Oregon | Great Plains |
| West Virginia | Washington (State) | New Mexico | South Dakota | Alaska |
| Rhode Island | Virginia | | Rocky Mountains | Wyoming |
| Indiana | California | Nevada | Wisconsin | Alabama |
| Delaware | Mississippi | Michigan | Arizona | Massachusetts |

# United States Geography Bingo

| Georgia | Oregon | Arizona | New York | Florida |
|---------|--------|---------|----------|---------|
| Maryland | Michigan | Washington (State) | Utah | Mississippi |
| Virginia | Idaho | | Great Plains | Oklahoma |
| Texas | Indiana | North Carolina | Tennessee | South Dakota |
| Colorado | Maine | Delaware | Wisconsin | West Virginia |

# United States Geography Bingo

| Michigan | Great Plains | Indiana | New Mexico | Maine |
|---|---|---|---|---|
| Vermont | Oklahoma | Nevada | Massachusetts | Arizona |
| New Hampshire | Washington (State) | | Alaska | New York |
| Rocky Mountains | West Virginia | Minnesota | Tennessee | South Dakota |
| Delaware | Louisiana | Wisconsin | California | Virginia |

# United States Geography Bingo

| Connecticut | New York | Utah | Maine | Great Plains |
|---|---|---|---|---|
| Alabama | Oregon | New Jersey | Mississippi | Alaska |
| Vermont | Iowa |  | U.S. Virgin Islands | Nevada |
| Wisconsin | California | Colorado | Tennessee | Rocky Mountains |
| West Virginia | Illinois | Virginia | Michigan | Arizona |

www.ingramcontent.com/pod-product-compliance
Lightning Source LLC
LaVergne TN
LVHW061336060426
835511LV00014B/1955